Start Writing
Amazing
Stories

Ruth Thomson

Belitha Press

First published in the UK in 2000 by

Belitha Press Ltd
London House, Great Eastern Wharf,
Parkgate Road, London SW11 4NQ

ISBN 1 84138 227 2 (hardback)
ISBN 1 84138 229 9 (paperback)

British Library in Publication Data for this book is available
from the British Library.

Series editors: Mary-Jane Wilkins, Stephanie Turnbull
Designers: Holly Mann, Rachel Hamdi
Illustrators: Colin Paine, Sara Walker and Gwyneth Williamson
Educational consultants: Pie Corbett, Poet and Consultant
  to the National Literacy Strategy; Sarah Mullen, Literacy Consultant

Printed in China

Contents

WRITING STORIES

In every part of the world, people have always told stories – to amuse and entertain one another, or to explain strange and unusual events.

There are six different stories for you to read. They retell traditional tales from many different places, including India, China and Russia. You can use them as models to create your own stories in similar styles.

Each story is followed by a plan like the one on the right. This helps you to write your own amazing story. It is divided into parts:

The story begins
This gives you a story topic to think about.

THE STORY BEGINS
Write your own version of the Stone Soup story. Here are some questions and ideas to help you.

THE CHARACTERS AND THE SETTING
★ Who is the main character?
Where does she or he go?

to a castle   to a palace   to a school kitchen

THE BUILD-UP
★ What is she or he carrying?

a suitcase   a trunk   a lunch box

★ What is inside?

a handful of rusty nails   a gold coin   a fishbone

★ What dish does your character decide to make?

a stew   a dessert   a pie

The characters and setting

First decide who the characters are and where they live. Are they old or young? Are they rich or poor? Give them names and think about what they are like.

The build-up

Now the action begins. It's up to you to choose what the characters do, where they go and what happens next.

THE TRICK
How does your character start making this dish?
What does she or he ask for to make it taste better? Choose three or four different foods.

peas   onions   tomatoes   spices   salt   pepper

chicken   garlic   cheese   sugar   butter   flour

lemon   chocolate   eggs   jam   apples   plums

THE RESOLUTION
When the dish is ready, what happens?

People eat it up.   People spit it out.   There is a big feast.

THE ENDING
What happens when the dish is finished?

What does the main character do?

What do the people tell their freinds?

13

The trick or conflict

In each story there is a trick, a problem or an unexpected event to think about. There are suggestions for what this might be.

The resolution

Now you can decide how to solve the conflicts and what might happen next.

Perhaps things turn out well...

...or very badly!

The ending

Readers always like to know how a story ends. Think about what happens to all the characters and describe how they feel. They may be angry or sorry, disappointed or relieved.

THE THREE WISHES

One night, a poor man and woman were sitting by the fireside grumbling.

'All our neighbours seem richer and happier than us,' said the woman. 'If only I could wish for anything I wanted, I know I would be happier than any of them.'

'Me too,' agreed the man. 'Wouldn't it be wonderful if a fairy came and gave us whatever we wanted!'

No sooner had he said these words than there was a bright flash. To their surprise, a sparkling fairy appeared by the fireplace.

'I overheard what you said,' smiled the fairy, 'and I have come to to give you three wishes. But take care – after these three wishes, you can't ever wish for anything more.'

The fairy disappeared, leaving the couple to decide on their wishes. The wife said, 'If it was up to me, I would wish for beauty, riches and goodness.'

The husband said, 'If it was up to me, I would wish for health, cheerfulness and a long life.'

'It's such a pity we've got only three wishes,' said the wife. 'Perhaps we should wait until morning to make up our minds.'

She added some coal to the fire as she talked. Without thinking, she said, 'What a nice fire. I wish we had a fish to fry on it for our supper.'

No sooner had she finished speaking than a large, silver fish came tumbling down the chimney.

'You silly wife!' exclaimed her husband. 'You've just wasted our first wish! I'm so cross with you that I wish the fish would stick to your nose.'

No sooner had he finished speaking than the fish jumped up and stuck fast to the end of the woman's nose. She tried to pull it off, but the fish would not budge.

'You silly husband!' exclaimed the wife, 'now you've wasted our second wish.'

'In that case, let's use our third wish to ask for riches,' said the man, 'then we could buy anything we wanted, including a gold case to hide the fish.'

'Certainly not,' said the woman. 'I don't want a fish dangling from my nose for the rest of my life.'

Before her husband could say another word, the wife quickly said, 'I wish this fish would drop off my nose.'

No sooner had she finished speaking than the fish dropped off her nose straight into her lap.

'Well, dear husband,' said the wife, 'our wishes didn't get us very far, did they? Perhaps that's a lesson to us to be happy with what we have. In the meantime, let's fry this fish for our supper, since that's the only thing left of our wishes.'

So the couple tucked into a good meal and never wished for anything more ever again.

THE STORY BEGINS

Write a story about three wishes, which ends back where it started. Here are some questions and ideas to help you.

THE CHARACTERS AND THE SETTING

★ Who are the characters? Why do they want three wishes? Where do they live?

in a cave

on a boat

at the top of a skyscraper

THE BUILD-UP

★ When the characters make their first wish, what happens?

They become famous.

They become rich.

They find themselves in a castle.

They become animals.

They become invisible.

They end up in a lost world.

THE CONFLICT

★ When they make their *second* wish, what happens?
Make something go wrong or happen unexpectedly.

★ Perhaps the characters are:

chased

tricked

lost

robbed

THE RESOLUTION

★ When the characters make their *third* wish, what happens?

Remember – the third wish should bring your story back
to where it started.

THE ENDING

★ How do the characters feel?

pleased
grateful
happy
relieved

disappointed
sad
upset
sorry

What do they say about their wishes?

STONE SOUP

One evening, a traveller called Peter arrived at a small village, carrying a large pot, a bundle of twigs and a bulging backpack. He busily made a fire with the twigs, filled the pot with water and put it on the fire to boil. Some of the villagers gathered to watch. They were astounded to see Peter take three smooth stones out of his backpack and put them into the pot.

'What are you doing?' asked a curious girl.

'Making stone soup,' replied Peter. 'It's a real delicacy. Mind you, it would taste even better with a handful of carrots and beans in it. Does anyone have a few to spare?'

One of the villagers ran to her house and came back with some carrots and beans. Peter cut them up and stirred them into the pot. Then he took a spoonful of soup and tasted it.

'Is it ready yet?' asked the curious girl.

'Not quite,' replied Peter. 'It's very tasty, but it could do with some potatoes to thicken it. Does anyone have a few to spare?'

A villager ran to her house and came back with some potatoes. Peter cut them up and put them in the pot.

Then he took a spoonful of soup and tasted it.

'Is it ready yet?' asked the curious girl.

'Not quite,' replied Peter.

'It's very delicious, but it could do with some herbs to bring out the full flavour of the stones. Does anyone have some to spare?'

A villager ran to his house and came back with a fistful of herbs. Peter cut them up and stirred them into his pot. Then he took a spoonful of the soup and tasted it.

'Is it ready yet?' asked the curious girl.

'Almost,' replied Peter. 'It just needs a pinch of salt and pepper to make it taste perfect. Does anyone have some to spare?

A villager ran to his house and came back with some salt and pepper. Peter stirred them into his pot. Then he tasted a spoonful of soup.

'Is it ready yet?' asked the curious girl.

'Yes!' replied Peter, triumphantly.

By now, all the villagers had gathered around the fire, each holding a bowl and spoon. Peter gave everyone a ladleful of his stone soup. Soon, there was nothing left in the pot except the three stones. Peter took them out, wiped them clean and put them into his backpack.

'What do you think of stone soup?' he asked with a smile.

The villagers told him that it was the best soup they had ever tasted. They talked about it long after Peter had left their village for the next one over the hill.

THE STORY BEGINS

Write your own version of the Stone Soup story.
Here are some questions and ideas to help you.

THE CHARACTERS AND THE SETTING

★ Who is the main character?
Where does she or he go?

to a castle

to a palace

to a school kitchen

THE BUILD-UP

★ What is she or he carrying?

a suitcase

a trunk

a lunch box

★ What is inside?

a handful of rusty nails

a gold coin

a fishbone

★ What dish does your character decide to make?

a stew

a dessert

a pie

THE TRICK

★ How does your character start making this dish?

★ What does she or he ask for to make it taste better?
Choose three or four different foods.

peas   onions   tomatoes   spices   salt   pepper

chicken   garlic   cheese   sugar   butter   flour

lemon   chocolate   eggs   jam   apples   plums

THE RESOLUTION

★ When the dish is ready, what happens?

People eat it up.

People spit it out.

There is a big feast.

THE ENDING

★ What happens when the dish
is finished?

What does the main character do?

What do the people tell their friends?

THE FOX AND THE STORK

One day Mr Fox invited his neighbour, Miss Stork, for dinner. Miss Stork was very flattered by this invitation. She spent all afternoon smoothing her feathers and polishing her beak. By the time evening came, she was very hungry and was looking forward to a tasty meal.

When Miss Stork arrived at Mr Fox's house, she took a delicate sniff.

'Something smells good,' she said to Mr Fox with a smile.

'Take a seat,' said Mr Fox, 'and I will bring you your dinner.'

Mr Fox went to the kitchen.

He came back with two bowls of steaming soup and put them on the table. He sat down beside Miss Stork and greedily started lapping up his soup. Miss Stork pecked this way and that, but however hard she tried, she could not drink the soup. Her narrow beak was far too long for the shallow bowl.

'Don't you like my soup?' grinned spiteful Mr Fox. 'Shall I have your helping?'

Mr Fox greedily lapped up Miss Stork's soup until there was none left. Miss Stork said nothing, but thanked him politely for her evening. But she flew home very hungry and cross that Mr Fox had played such a nasty trick on her.

The following week, Miss Stork invited Mr Fox for dinner. Mr Fox was very pleased with this invitation. He spent all afternoon cleaning his fur and brushing his tail. By the time evening came, he was starving and couldn't wait for a delicious dinner.

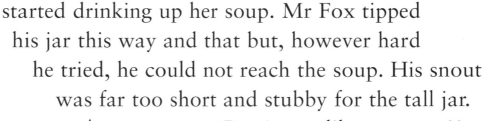

When he arrived at Miss Stork's house, Mr Fox took a deep sniff.

'Something smells tasty,' he said to Miss Stork with a grin.

'Do sit down,' said Miss Stork. 'Dinner is almost ready.'

Miss Stork went to the kitchen. She came back with two tall jars of steaming soup and put them on the table. She sat down beside Mr Fox and started drinking up her soup. Mr Fox tipped his jar this way and that but, however hard he tried, he could not reach the soup. His snout was far too short and stubby for the tall jar.

'Don't you like my soup?' smiled clever Miss Stork. 'Shall I have your helping?'

Quick as a flash, she drank all Mr Fox's soup.

This time it was Mr Fox who went home hungry and cross.

'That will teach him,' said Miss Stork to herself as she shut the door behind Mr Fox. 'If you play mean tricks on people, they may play them back on you.'

THE STORY BEGINS

Write a story about a trick that Mr Fox plays on another animal.
Here are some questions and ideas to help you.

THE CHARACTERS

★ Who will Mr Fox play his trick on? It could be:

a frog

a hen

a bear

a giraffe

THE BUILD-UP

★ What food does Mr Fox make?

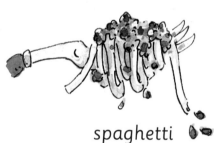

spaghetti

peas

pizza

chewy toffees

THE TRICK

★ How does Mr Fox serve the food?

Choose something that the animal could not eat from.
It might be:

a flat plate

a deep bowl

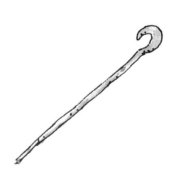

a tall glass

a long skewer

THE RESOLUTION

★ Think of a way for the animal to get its own back on Mr Fox.
It could be:

taking him for a ride
in a leaky boat

leading him
to a hive of bees

making him
fall in the mud

giving him
a bowl of sawdust

locking him
in a shed

making him
climb a tall tree

THE ENDING

★ What does the animal say?

What does Mr Fox say and do?

SIX BLIND MEN AND THE ELEPHANT

There were once six blind men who lived in a small village in India. They sat in the shade of a huge tree all day long, discussing anything and everything. One day there was great excitement because an elephant had wandered into the village.

'What's an elephant like?' asked one of the blind men when he heard the news.

None of the others knew, so they decided to go and find out.

The first man felt the elephant's trunk, which squirmed and twisted in his hands.

'Aha,' he said to himself. 'Now I know what an elephant is like. It's long and wriggly.'

The second man felt one of the elephant's smooth tusks. Its point dug into his hands.

'Aha,' he said to himself. 'Now I know what an elephant is like. It's sharp and pointed.'

The third man felt one of the elephant's huge, flapping ears.

'Aha,' he said to himself. 'Now I know what an elephant is like. It's thin and smooth.'

The fourth man felt the elephant's thick, round leg.

'Aha,' he said to himself. 'Now I know what an elephant is like. It's hard and knobbly.'

The fifth man felt up and down and all along the rough, solid side of the elephant's body.

'Aha,' he said to himself. 'Now I know what an elephant is like. It's strong and firm.'

The sixth man felt the elephant's wiry tail. 'Aha,' he said to himself, 'Now I know what an elephant is like. It's thin and hairy.'

The six blind men compared what they had felt. Of course, they couldn't agree at all.

The first man said that an elephant was like a long snake. The second man disagreed, saying it was like a sharp knife. The third man interrupted and said that it was like a flapping fan. The fourth man laughed and said it was like a strong tree trunk. The fifth man argued that it was like a high wall and the sixth man said that it was like a thin rope.

The men started to shout and fight with one another.

'Ahem,' the elephant interrupted loudly, 'I wonder if I could say something.' The blind men stopped shouting and fighting to listen.

'All of you are wrong,' said the elephant, 'but all of you are right. I am an enormous animal with many different parts. My wriggly trunk is like a snake. My sharp tusks are like knives. My flapping ears are like fans. My strong legs are like tree trunks, my huge body is like a wall and my thin tail is like a rope.'

The men laughed to think how silly they had been. They took turns to feel every single part of the elephant, so they could discover what it was like all over.

THE STORY BEGINS

Write a story about six blind men meeting another animal.
Here are some questions and ideas to help you.

THE ANIMAL AND THE SETTING

★ Decide which animal the blind men are going to feel.
Choose an animal with an interesting shape, for example:

a crocodile

a camel

a giraffe

a wolf

a flamingo

a kangaroo

★ Where do the blind men find their animal?

in a forest

near a swamp

in a cave

by a river

up a mountain

in a desert

20

THE BUILD-UP AND THE CONFLICT

★ The blind men disagree about what the animal is like.
What does each one compare the animal with?

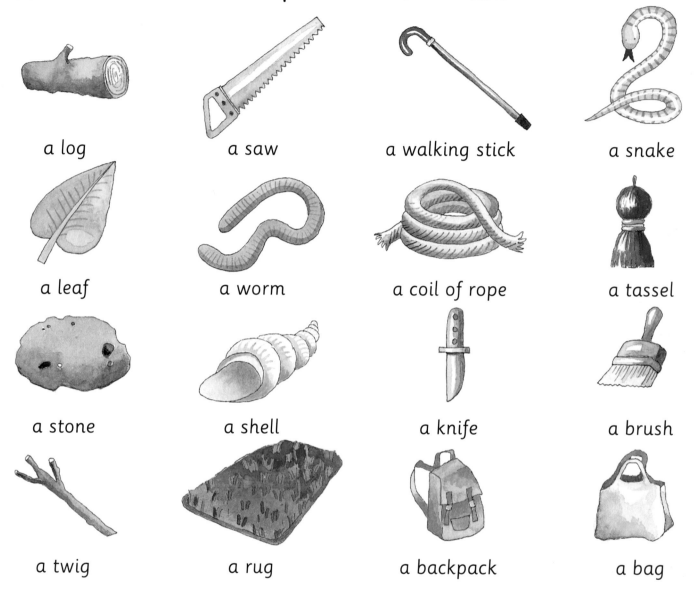

a log

a saw

a walking stick

a snake

a leaf

a worm

a coil of rope

a tassel

a stone

a shell

a knife

a brush

a twig

a rug

a backpack

a bag

THE RESOLUTION

★ What might happen next? Perhaps the animal ...

eats the blind men   chases them   talks to them

THE ENDING

★ What happens in the end to both
the blind men and the animal?

THE MONKEY AND THE CROCODILE

Monkey lived in a tall tree beside a wide river, deep in the jungle. He spent his time scampering from branch to branch and feeding on berries. His greatest friend was Crocodile, who spent his days swimming in the river or lazing in the sunshine on the bank near Monkey's tree. Every day, kind Monkey threw some berries down to Crocodile, who ate them all up.

One day, Monkey threw down an extra large helping of berries and told Crocodile to give some to his wife. Crocodile's wife thought the berries were a very delicious gift indeed. When she heard that Monkey ate nothing but these berries, she thought greedily that Monkey himself would make a very tasty dinner. She knew that her husband would never agree to harm Monkey, so she hatched a wicked plot.

She went to bed, pretending to be ill, and moaned, 'Husband, dear husband, I am weak and sick! Only Monkey's heart can give me strength.'

Crocodile didn't know what to do. He loved his wife and wanted to help her, but he was best friends with Monkey and didn't want to hurt him.

Meanwhile, his wife kept moaning and groaning and looking pale.

'Husband, dear husband,' she groaned, 'If I don't have Monkey's heart, I will die. Please invite Monkey for dinner.'

Crocodile was very upset. He didn't want to trick Monkey, but he didn't want his wife to die, so in the end he agreed. He invited Monkey to dinner, just as his wife had asked. Monkey, pleased with the invitation, jumped down from the branches and climbed on to Crocodile's back.

Crocodile set off across the river to his home. Halfway across, he began to dive underwater.

'Stop, stop!' cried Monkey in alarm. 'I can't swim. I shall drown.'

'That's the idea,' grinned foolish Crocodile, blurting out his secret. 'My wife is ill and says that only your heart can cure her.'

'My heart!' exclaimed Monkey, thinking very quickly. 'Why didn't you say so sooner? I keep my heart hidden in a hole in my tree. If you swim back there, I can go and fetch it for your wife.'

Silly Crocodile believed clever Monkey's lie. Anxious to get Monkey's heart as soon as possible, he hurriedly turned around and swam back to Monkey's tree. As soon as they reached the river bank, Monkey leapt ashore and scampered up the tree, well out of reach of Crocodile.

'Thank your wife for her kind dinner invitation,' Monkey shouted down from the treetops, 'but I have changed my mind, now that I can see what sort of friend you are. I shall stay here and enjoy a feast of berries.'

Crocodile swam away sadly. He realized that he had been outwitted and that he had lost his greatest friend.

THE STORY BEGINS

Write your own story about two friends who become enemies. Here are some questions and ideas to help you.

THE CHARACTERS AND THE SETTING

★ Choose two very different characters – one should be a fierce hunter and the other gentle and kind.

Decide where they might live. They could be:

an eagle and a rabbit living in the mountains   a cat and a mouse living in a house   a child and a lion living on a grassy plain

THE BUILD-UP

★ How do the characters spend their time?

playing   swimming   exploring   lazing about

★ What does the kind character give the hunter?

fish   sweets   bones   cheese   fur

THE CONFLICT

★ The hunter wants to eat the kind character.
What trick does he play to capture him? He might:

build a trap

invite him to lunch

give him a fake present

pretend to be asleep

THE RESOLUTION

★ When the gentle character discovers he has been tricked,
what does he do? He might:

make his own trap

tie up the hunter

hide somewhere safe

call for his friends

THE ENDING

★ What does the gentle character say to the hunter?

How does the hunter feel?

THE MAGIC BRUSH

ong ago in China there lived a boy named Ma Liang, who loved drawing. He was too poor to buy a brush, so he drew on the ground with a twig or scratched pictures on walls with a sharp stone.

One night, when Ma Liang was fast asleep, an old man woke him with a gentle tap. Ma Liang looked at him in astonishment.

'I can see you love drawing,' said the old man, 'so I have brought you a magic brush. Use it to help the poor people in your village.'

With that, the old man disappeared. Excitedly, Ma Liang tried out his new brush. He drew a picture of a bird on the wall. It changed at once into a real bird, which flapped its wings and flew away. Ma Liang was thrilled.

When morning came, he went out with his brush to find out what the villagers needed. The first person he saw was a tired man pulling a plough.

'You need an ox to help you plough,' said Ma Liang. He drew an ox on the ground and it changed into a real ox. Next he saw a woman pulling up weeds.

'You need a hoe to help you pull up weeds,' said Ma Liang and drew a hoe on a stone. It changed into a real hoe. Every day Ma Liang drew things people needed.

It wasn't long before the powerful emperor heard about Ma Liang's magic brush. He sent his soldiers to capture Ma Liang and bring him to the palace.

'Draw me a tree covered with gold,' ordered the emperor.

Ma Liang did not want to obey the greedy ruler so, instead, he painted a calm sea with a small island in the distance. At once this changed into real sea and a real island.

'Where is my tree covered with gold?' asked the emperor angrily.

'Here,' said Ma Liang, drawing a golden tree on the island. It changed into a real tree, glistening with gold.

'Draw me a boat to get to the island,' demanded the emperor furiously.

Ma Liang drew a boat. It changed into a real boat. The emperor climbed aboard. Ma Liang drew a puff of wind to blow the boat to the island. Real wind blew and the boat set sail.

'This wind isn't strong enough,' shouted the emperor impatiently. 'Draw some stronger wind.'

Ma Liang drew some stronger wind. As the wind blew, the waves became rougher. They rose so high that they washed over the boat and capsized it. The greedy emperor disappeared beneath the waves, never to be seen again.

Ma Liang drew himself a horse, which turned into a real horse.

He galloped home to his village to tell everyone what had happened.

THE STORY BEGINS

Write your own story about a magic brush.
Here are some questions and ideas to help you.

THE CHARACTERS AND THE SETTING

★ Imagine you are the hero or heroine of this story.
Where do you live?

THE BUILD-UP

★ One night, someone gives you a magic brush …
Who is it?

a wizard   a fairy   a cat   a genie

★ What do you draw with the brush?

★ Someone hears about the magic brush and kidnaps you.
Who is it?

a cruel queen   a greedy family   a jealous magician   a sneaky thief

THE CONFLICT

★ What are you told to draw?

a treasure chest

a lion

a feast

a fast car

★ Do you do as you are told? What might you do instead?

THE RESOLUTION

★ Early next morning, you decide to get away ...
What could you draw to help you escape?

a helicopter

a speed boat

a horse

a submarine

★ What could you draw to stop anyone catching you?

thick fog

locked gates

a deep hole

a wide river

THE ENDING

★ How does your story end?

Where do you go?

Do you tell anyone what happened?

WRITING TIPS

Here are some useful tips to help you start writing all kinds of amazing stories.

What do I need?

You need plenty of paper, or maybe a notebook and a pencil or pen. Coloured pencils or felt tips will be useful for your illustrations. Most writers like to have a quiet place where they can write.

How do I choose a title?

You may want to use the story titles given in this book, or you may have some better ideas yourself. Do not worry too much about the title. Sometimes it is easier to think of a title after you have written the story. Try to make the title sound exciting.

How do I start my story?

Once you have thought what is going to happen in your story you need to write a thrilling opening. Here are some ideas.

• Start with an unusual event – The genie hovered right in front of me...

• or with an interesting setting – I peered into the dark, gloomy cave...

• or with somebody speaking – 'What's that strange noise?' asked Tom.

How do I make my characters sound real?

Describe the way your characters look or move or talk, giving each one different characteristics. Decide how they might be feeling or what they might be thinking. This will help you think about what the characters say or do next.

You could base characters on people that you know well (though perhaps you should not tell them this – especially if they end up as baddies!).

What should I write about?

In this book there are lots of suggestions for the main problem your characters might face. You could use one of these or think of a completely different idea.

Build your story around the problem that the characters have to solve.

How do I work out what happens?

It can help to talk your ideas through with a friend. Some people like to draw a series of little pictures – a bit like a cartoon strip – to help decide what will happen in their story.

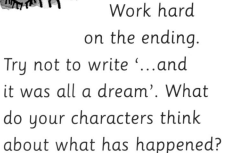

You need to have an idea of how the tale will end. You can always change this if you have a better idea as you write. Work hard on the ending. Try not to write '...and it was all a dream'. What do your characters think about what has happened?

What else can I do?

Now you can add illustrations or even make a cover. Don't forget to put your name on it. You are the author!